M000049956

FOR GOD HAS NOT GIVEN US
A SPIRIT OF FEAR, BUT OF
power and of love
AND OF A SOUND MIND.

— 2 TIMOTHY 1:7 (NKJV)

You are my refuge

AND MY SHIELD;
YOUR WORD IS MY
SOURCE OF HOPE.

— PSALM 119:114 (NLT)

don't BOAST about tomorrow

ABOVE ALL, CLOTHE YOURSELVES WITH LOVE, WHICH BINDS US ALL TOGETHER IN *perfect harmony.*

— COLOSSIANS 3:14 (NLT)

I have said this to you,
that in me you may have
peace. In the world you
have tribulation; but be
of good cheer, I have
overcome the world.

— JOHN 16:33 (RSV)

MY FLESH AND MY HEART
MAY FAIL, BUT
God is the strength
OF MY HEART AND
MY PORTION FOR EVER.

— PSALM 73:26 (RSV)

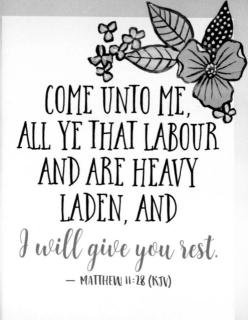

COME UNTO ME,
ALL YE THAT LABOUR
AND ARE HEAVY
LADEN, AND
I will give you rest.

— MATTHEW 11:28 (KJV)

FINALLY, MY BRETHREN,
BE STRONG IN THE LORD,
AND IN THE
power of his might.

— EPHESIANS 6:10 (KJV)

And after you have
suffered a little while,
the God of all grace,
who has called you to
his eternal glory
in Christ, will himself
restore, establish,
and strengthen you.

— 1 PETER 5:10 (RSV)

THE SOVEREIGN Lord
IS MY STRENGTH; HE MAKES
MY FEET LIKE THE FEET OF A
DEER, HE ENABLES ME TO
*tread on
the heights.*

— HABAKKUK 3:19 (NIV)

Glorious are you, More Majestic THAN the MouNtains

Dear brothers and sisters,
when troubles of any kind
come your way, consider it
an opportunity for great joy.
For you know that when your
faith is tested, your endurance
has a chance to grow.

— JAMES 1:2-3 (NLT)

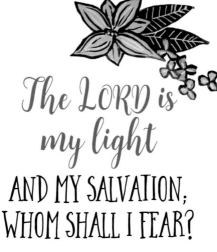

The LORD is
my light
AND MY SALVATION;
WHOM SHALL I FEAR?

— PSALM 27:1 (NRSV)

We are troubled on every side, yet not distressed; we are perplexed, but not in despair; persecuted, but not forsaken; *cast down, but not destroyed.*

— 2 CORINTHIANS 4:8-9 (KJV)

Let us also lay aside every weight, and sin which clings so closely, and let us *run with perseverance* the race that is set before us.

— HEBREWS 12:1 (RSV)

THE Lord WILL
GIVE STRENGTH UNTO
HIS PEOPLE; THE Lord
WILL BLESS HIS PEOPLE

with peace.

— PSALM 29:11 (KJV)

THEREFORE,
MY DEAR BROTHERS
AND SISTERS,
stand firm.
LET NOTHING
MOVE YOU.

— 1 CORINTHIANS 15:58 (NIV)

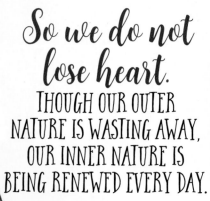

So we do not lose heart. THOUGH OUR OUTER NATURE IS WASTING AWAY, OUR INNER NATURE IS BEING RENEWED EVERY DAY.

— 2 CORINTHIANS 4:16 (RSV)

Be of good courage,

AND HE SHALL STRENGTHEN YOUR HEART, ALL YE THAT HOPE IN THE LORD.

— PSALM 31:24 (KJV)

A cheerful
heart is a good
medicine.

— PROVERBS 17:22 (RSV)

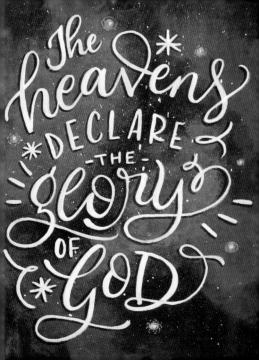

Rejoice in your hope,

BE PATIENT IN TRIBULATION, BE CONSTANT IN PRAYER.

— ROMANS 12:12 (RSV)

For whatever was written in former days was written for our instruction, that by steadfastness and by the encouragement of *the scriptures we might have hope.*

— ROMANS 15:4 (RSV)

NOW MAY THE GOD OF HOPE
FILL YOU WITH ALL JOY AND
peace in believing,
THAT YOU MAY ABOUND
IN HOPE BY THE POWER
OF THE HOLY SPIRIT.

— ROMANS 15:13 (NKJV)

Surely God is my salvation; I WILL TRUST AND NOT BE AFRAID.

— ISAIAH 12:2 (NIV)

When you pass
through the waters,
I will be with you;
and when you pass through
the rivers, they will not
sweep over you. When you
walk through the fire,
you will not be burned;
the flames will not set
you ablaze.

— ISAIAH 43:2 (NIV)

Finally, brethren,
farewell. Be perfect,
be of good comfort,
be of one mind, live in
peace; and the God
of love and peace
shall be with you.

— 2 CORINTHIANS 13:11 (KJV)

JESUS SAID TO HIM,
"I am the way,
THE TRUTH, AND THE LIFE.
NO ONE COMES TO THE FATHER
EXCEPT THROUGH ME."

— JOHN 14:6 (NKJV)

AND SO WE KNOW AND
RELY ON THE LOVE GOD
HAS FOR US.

God is love.

WHOEVER LIVES IN LOVE
LIVES IN GOD,
AND GOD IN THEM.

— 1 JOHN 4:16 (NIV)

Dear children,
LET US NOT LOVE
WITH WORDS OR SPEECH
BUT WITH ACTIONS
AND IN TRUTH.

— 1 JOHN 3:18 (NIV)

IT IS MORE *blessed* TO GIVE THAN TO RECEIVE.

— ACTS 20:35 (NKJV)

LOOK AT THOSE WHO
ARE HONEST AND GOOD,
FOR A WONDERFUL FUTURE
AWAITS THOSE WHO

love peace.

— PSALM 37: 37 (NLT)

Ask,

AND IT WILL BE GIVEN
TO YOU; SEEK, AND YOU
WILL FIND; KNOCK,
AND IT WILL BE
OPENED TO YOU.

— MATTHEW 7:7 (NKJV)

So I concluded there is nothing better than to be happy and enjoy ourselves as long as we can. And people should eat and drink and enjoy the fruits of their labor, for these are *gifts from God.*

— ECCLESIASTES 3:12-13 (NLT)

Blessed are the pure

in heart, for they
shall see God.
Blessed are the
peacemakers,
for they shall be
called sons of God.

— MATTHEW 5:8-9 (RSV)

⁴lest they drink and forget what has been decreed,
  and deprive all the oppressed of their rights.
⁶Let beer be for those who are perishing,
  wine for those who are in anguish!
⁷Let them drink and forget their poverty
  and remember their misery no more.

⁸Speak up for those who cannot speak for themselves,
  for the rights of all who are destitute.
⁹Speak up and judge fairly;
  defend the rights of the poor and needy.

Epilogue: The Wife of Noble Character

¹⁰A wife of noble character who can find?
  She is worth far more than rubies.
¹¹Her husband has full confidence in her
  and lacks nothing of value.
¹²She brings him good, not harm,
  all the days of her life.
¹³She selects wool and flax
  and works with eager hands.
¹⁴She is like the merchant ships,
  bringing her food from afar.
¹⁵She gets up while it is still night;
  she provides food for her family
  and portions for her female servants.
¹⁶She considers a field and buys it;
  out of her earnings she plants a vineyard.
¹⁷She sets about her work vigorously;
  her arms are strong for her tasks.
¹⁸She sees that her trading is profitable,
  and her lamp does not go out at night.
¹⁹In her hand she holds the distaff
  and grasps the spindle with her fingers.
²⁰She opens her arms to the poor
  and extends her hands to the needy.
²¹When it snows, she has no fear for her household;
  for all of them are clothed in scarlet.
²²She makes coverings for her bed;
  she is clothed in fine linen and purple.
²³Her husband is respected at the city gate,
  where he takes his seat among the elders of the land.
²⁴She makes linen garments and sells them,
  and supplies the merchants with sashes.
²⁵She is clothed with strength and dignity;
  she can laugh at the days to come.
²⁶She speaks with wisdom,
  and faithful instruction is on her tongue.
²⁷She watches over the affairs of her household
  and does not eat the bread of idleness.
²⁸Her children arise and call her blessed;
  her husband also, and he praises her:

²⁹ ...rses 10–31 are an acrostic poem, the verses of which begin...

LET ALL THAT YOU DO BE DONE
in love.

— 1 CORINTHIANS 16:14 (RSV)

Be strong

and of good courage,
do not fear or be in
dread of them:
for it is the LORD your
God who goes with you;
he will not fail you
or forsake you.

— DEUTERONOMY 31:6 (RSV)

YOUR WORD IS A LAMP TO GUIDE MY FEET AND A LIGHT

for my path.

— PSALM 119:105 (NLT)

THIS IS THE DAY THE Lord HAS MADE.

We will rejoice and be glad in it.

— PSALM 118:24 (NLT)

THEREFORE
do not worry
about tomorrow,
FOR TOMORROW WILL
WORRY ABOUT ITSELF.
EACH DAY HAS ENOUGH
TROUBLE OF ITS OWN.

— MATTHEW 6:34 (NIV)

The LORD is my rock,
and my fortress, and
my deliverer, my God,
my rock, in whom I take
refuge, my shield,
and the horn
of my salvation,
my stronghold.

— PSALM 18:2 (RSV)

If you are wise and understand God's ways, prove it by living an honorable life, doing good works with the *humility that comes from wisdom.*

— JAMES 3:13 (NLT)

Do not be anxious

about anything, but in every
situation, by prayer
and petition, with
thanksgiving, present
your requests to God.
And the peace of God,
which transcends all
understanding, will guard
your hearts and your
minds in Christ Jesus.

— PHILIPPIANS 4:6-7 (NIV)

"For I know the plans I have for you," says the LORD. "They are plans for good and not for disaster, to give you a future and a hope."

— JEREMIAH 29:11 (NLT)

And now, dear brothers and sisters, one final thing. Fix your thoughts on what is true, and honorable, and right, and pure, and lovely, and admirable. Think about things that are excellent and *worthy of praise.*

— PHILIPPIANS 4:8 (NLT)

For with God nothing shall be impossible.

— LUKE 1:37 (KJV)

Now faith

IS THE ASSURANCE OF THINGS HOPED FOR, THE CONVICTION OF THINGS NOT SEEN.

— HEBREWS 11:1 (RSV)

God blesses

those who patiently
endure testing and
temptation. Afterward
they will receive
the crown of life that
God has promised to
those who love him.

— JAMES 1:12 (NLT)

²From the ends of the earth I call to you,
 I call as my heart grows faint;
 lead me to the rock[m] that is higher than I.
³For you have been my refuge,[n]
 a strong tower against the foe.

⁴I long to dwell[o] in your tent forever
 and take refuge in the shelter of your wings.[p]
⁵For you, God, have heard my vows;[q]
 you have given me the heritage of those who fear
 your name.[r]

⁶Increase the days of the king's life,
 his years for many generations.[s]
⁷May he be enthroned in God's presence forever;[t]
 appoint your love and faithfulness to protect him.[u]

⁸Then I will ever sing in praise of your name[w]
 and fulfill my vows day after day.

Psalm 62[a]

For the director of music. For Jeduthun. A psalm of David.

¹Truly my soul finds rest[c] in God;
 my salvation comes from him.
²Truly he is my rock[y] and my salvation;
 he is my fortress, I will never be shaken.

³How long will you assault me?
 Would all of you throw me down —
 this leaning wall,[z] this tottering fence?
⁴Surely they intend to topple me
 from my lofty place;
 they take delight in lies.
With their mouths they bless,
 but in their hearts they curse.[A]

⁵Yes, my soul, find rest in God;
 my hope comes from him.
⁶Truly he is my rock and my salvation;
 he is my fortress, I will not be shaken.
⁷My salvation and my honor depend on God;[d]
 he is my mighty rock, my refuge.
⁸Trust in him at all times, you people;
 pour out your hearts to him,
 for God is our refuge.

⁹Surely the lowborn are but a breath,[e]
 the highborn are but a lie.
If weighed on a balance,[f] they are nothing;
 together they are only a breath.
¹⁰Do not trust in extortion
 or put vain hope in stolen goods;[g]
 though your riches increase,

And do not be conformed to this world, but be transformed by the renewing of your mind, that you may prove what *is* that good and acceptable and *perfect will of God.*

— ROMANS 12:2 (NKJV)

Be watchful,
STAND FIRM IN
YOUR FAITH,
BE COURAGEOUS,
BE STRONG.

— 1 CORINTHIANS 16:13 (RSV)

But those who
hope in the LORD will
renew their strength.
They will
*soar on wings
like eagles;*
they will run and not
grow weary, they will
walk and not be faint.

— ISAIAH 40:31 (NIV)

THE LORD IS MY STRENGTH AND SONG, AND HE IS BECOME MY *salvation.*

— EXODUS 15:2 (KJV)

BUT THE FRUIT OF THE SPIRIT IS
love, joy, peace,
forbearance, kindness,
goodness, faithfulness,
gentleness and
self-control.
AGAINST SUCH THINGS
THERE IS NO LAW.

— Galatians 5:22-23 (NIV)

GOD IS OUR
refuge and
strength,
AN EVER-PRESENT
HELP IN TROUBLE.

— PSALM 46:1 (NIV)

AND WE KNOW THAT IN ALL
THINGS GOD WORKS FOR THE
GOOD OF THOSE WHO LOVE HIM,
WHO HAVE BEEN CALLED

according to

his purpose.

— ROMANS 8:28 (NIV)

I can do
all things
in him who
strengthens
me.

— PHILIPPIANS 4:13 (RSV)

Be still,
AND KNOW
THAT I AM GOD.
I AM EXALTED AMONG
THE NATIONS,
I AM EXALTED
IN THE EARTH!

— PSALM 46:10 (RSV)

Let your light so shine

BEFORE MEN, THAT THEY
MAY SEE YOUR GOOD WORKS
AND GLORIFY YOUR
FATHER IN HEAVEN.

— MATTHEW 5:16 (NKJV)

The LORD is
my shepherd:
I shall not want.
He maketh me to lie down
in green pastures: he leadeth
me beside the still waters.
He restoreth my soul:
he leadeth me in the paths
of righteousness for
his name's sake.

— PSALM 23:1-3 (KJV)

Love is patient and kind; love is not jealous or boastful; it is not arrogant or rude. Love does not insist on its own way; it is not irritable or resentful; it does not rejoice at wrong, but rejoices in the right. Love bears all things, believes all things, hopes all things, endures all things.

— 1 CORINTHIANS 13:4-7 (RSV)

The LORD bless you and keep you;

The LORD make His face
shine upon you,
And be gracious to you;
The LORD lift up His
countenance upon you,
And give you peace.

— NUMBERS 6:24–26 (NKJV)

WE HAVE THIS AS A
SURE AND STEADFAST
anchor of the soul,
A HOPE THAT ENTERS
INTO THE INNER SHRINE
BEHIND THE CURTAIN.

— HEBREWS 6:19 (RSV)

Do to others
AS YOU WOULD
HAVE THEM
DO TO YOU.

— LUKE 6:31 (NIV)

SO LET'S NOT GET TIRED
*of doing what
is good.*

AT JUST THE RIGHT
TIME WE WILL REAP A
HARVEST OF BLESSING IF
we don't give up.

— GALATIANS 6:9 (NLT)

Peace I leave with you,
MY PEACE I GIVE TO YOU;
NOT AS THE WORLD GIVES
DO I GIVE TO YOU. LET NOT
YOUR HEART BE TROUBLED,
neither let it be afraid.

— JOHN 14:27 (NKJV)

Do nothing

from selfishness or
conceit, but in humility
count others better
than yourselves.
Let each of you look
not only to his own
interests, but also to
the interests of others.

— PHILIPPIANS 2:3-4 (RSV)

WHEN SHE SPEAKS,
her words
are wise,
AND SHE GIVES
INSTRUCTIONS
with kindness.

— PROVERBS 31:26 (NLT)

and tribulations, and at times, we find anxiety on the rise. That is when we need a reminder to focus on faith, not fear, and to use challenges to cultivate strength and to grow in our spiritual awareness.

Let this little book remind you of that inner strength and dignity. Carry it with you, and reach for it when you need it the most. Carefully chosen scripture inspires reflection and reminds us to practice truth every day as we strive to be a light in our families, communities, and the world.

She is clothed with strength and dignity, AND SHE LAUGHS WITHOUT FEAR OF THE FUTURE.

— PROVERBS 31:25

Title scripture is from NLT: The Holy Bible, New Living Translation

This little devotional encourages women of faith to take a spiritual time out, reminding us to operate from the strength of God's grace and love. Life may serve up trials

She is clothed
WITH
strength
AND dignity

To those who love peace

Designed by Margaret Rubiano
Illustrations © 2019 Megan Wells

Copyright © 2019
Peter Pauper Press, Inc.
202 Mamaroneck Avenue
White Plains, NY 10601 USA
All rights reserved
ISBN 978-1-4413-3158-8
Printed in China

7 6 5 4 3 2 1

Visit us at www.peterpauper.com

She is clothed
WITH
strength
AND dignity

Compiled by Barbara Paulding

Illustrated by Megan Wells

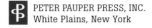

PETER PAUPER PRESS, INC.
White Plains, New York